Also by Dr. Carolyn Edwards

Teach Online. Ten Simple Steps to Get Your Resume Noticed and Land the Job

I Look Good, I Feel Good, I Am Good. The Woman's Guide to Love, Peace, and Happiness

Children's Books
Fun with Money
I Can Be Anything I Dream

SUNDAY
— AIN'T —
ENOUGH

SUNDAY
— AIN'T —
ENOUGH

A Devotional

DR. CAROLYN EDWARDS
Sunday Ain't Enough, LLC Miami FL

Publisher's *Note*

This publication is designed to provide accurate and authoritative information in regard to the subject matter covered. It is sold with the understanding that the publisher is not engaged in rendering psychological, financial, legal, or other professional services. If expert assistance or counseling is needed, the services of a competent professional should be sought.

A publication of Sunday Ain't Enough, LLC
Copyright 2023 by   Dr. Carolyn Edwards
                        Sunday Ain't Enough, LLC
                        Miami, FL 33157
                        www.drcarolynedwards.com

ISBN 978-0-9727040-8-3

Library of Congress Cataloging-in-Publication
Edwards, Carolyn Dr.
Sunday Ain't Enough a Devotional
Spiritual Life | Christianity | Spirituality | Prayer | Devotional

Scripture quotations are taken from the Holy Bible, New International Version, unless otherwise noted. Other bible versions used are the Common English Bible (CEB), Contemporary English Version (CEV), English Standard Version (ESV), King James Version (KJ), The Message (MSG), New Century Version (NCV), New International Reader's Version (NIRV), New King James Version (NKJV), New Living Translation (NLT), and New Live Version (NLV).

SUNDAY

—— AIN'T ——

ENOUGH

Also by Dr. Carolyn Edwards

Teach Online. Ten Simple Steps to Get Your Resume Noticed and Land the Job

I Look Good, I Feel Good, I Am Good. The Woman's Guide to Love, Peace, and Happiness

Children's Books
Fun with Money
I Can Be Anything I Dream

To my Father, God, who never gives up on me. I finally know that living my life boldly and unapologetically in nonconformity as Your original one-of-a-kind creation is the reason why I am here.

To each reader, thank you for taking this ride with me. May God bless you tremendously as you grow to love Him, love people, and love you. I love you all!

Don't become so well-adjusted to your culture that you fit into it without even thinking. Instead fix your attention on God.

Romans 12:2 MSG

CONTENTS

INTRODUCTION

Every day is an opportunity to talk to God, walk with God, hear from God, enjoy God, be close to God, and appreciate God as you experience his love, peace, joy, power, protection, and direction. God has already given you everything you need to live an amazing life of joy and purpose, but Sunday Ain't Enough to build a wonderfully enjoyable life of faith where you trust God for everything.

It's really hard to trust someone you don't know, so in each devotion, you will find a spiritual boost to get you moving in the right direction of knowing God, loving God, and loving you. I promise as God spoke to me so I could present it to you, I needed the same lessons for my life, growth, and spiritual development.

I am in this with you. Knowing God, your father, your creator should be easy, clear, and simple an exciting adventure that unfolds which is my purpose for writing….to help everyone trust God in everything. However, I want you to know a few hours in church on Sunday, a quick prayer over your food, or watching a few short clips and reels during the week ain't enough to know God, love God, appreciate God or know all the lessons, blessings, power, help, abundance, peace, healing, joy, kindness, and love He has waiting for you.

Building a relationship with God does not happen overnight, and life does not happen in a straight line, so feel free to make a left, right, or U-turn to the page that speaks to your heart. You are free so go at your own pace while you take the limitations off what you think God can do. God can do

1

more than you could ever think, dream, or imagine in ways no one has ever seen. Love, real love, is waiting for you in this easy to read and use devotional. Just three simple yet powerful steps to get you moving in the right direction:

Step 1 Scripture – God's word

Step 2 Devotional – God's work

Step 3 Prayer – God's help

As you read and reflect, listen for His voice, and in the space that follows each prayer, write down your thoughts, prayers, and dreams as well as God speaks to your heart.

God absolutely makes no mistakes. You belong to God and He hears your prayers. Allow this truth to guide your thoughts and your actions. Remember there is never a time God is not God, there is never a time God's word is not true, there is never a time you are not loved, there is never a time you do not have a purpose for living, there is never a time anyone can take your place, there is never a time someone can steal your blessing, and there is never a time God will give up on you. God will always get you where you need to be.

Make every day an adventure because the best is yet to come!

Peace and blessings,

Dr. Carolyn

PART I

GOD IS

God is the I AM.
Exodus 3:14
King eternal, immortal, invisible.
1 Timothy 1:17
From forever in the past to forever in the future.
Psalm 90:2

God is the creator of all things, heaven, and earth, seen and unseen. He is the ever-present help in times of trouble who never keeps track of how many times you ask or how many times you run backwards when he calls you to move forward. He gives generously without faulting you for anything. He is always gentle, always kind and always lovingly guiding you on the right track.

Although God's characteristics are innumerable and infinite, He reveals Himself to you, so you know him. Even though the world and situations change, God's character never does. He is always good, always giving, and always loving!

Before you read the devotions in this section, put **"God is"** in front of the title to help you know God, love God, and trust God with everything.

4

ALL KNOWING

How great is our Lord! His power is absolute!
His understanding is beyond comprehension!
Psalm 147:5 NLT

I like the exclamations used in this scripture because they show strong emotions. It is as if the scripture is saying you better not take God for granted. You better stop and recognize! God is all that, period! No further explanation needed. That is all.

God is omniscient, which means He knows everything about everything. His understanding is so much more than you can ever wrap your mind around that we cannot fully comprehend who He is or His ways. Although you can't figure it out, trust me, He knows all about you. He knows the good, the bad, and the ugly. The beginning, the middle, and the end of your story.

You might think God doesn't know everything, but He knows even the number of hairs in your head. He doesn't judge you even though He knows all the questionable behavior or not-so-smart things you've done. Like the times you've dimmed your light to fit in with people, in places and spaces that were less than what God wanted for you. How about the times you did not like and love you or appreciate all He created and called you to be? Don't feel bad, I've been there too. Just know there is there is nothing you are going through that God does not know about. The Bible says in Proverbs 18:24, *"He is a friend that sticks closer than a brother."* This means God not only

5

loves you, but His love is genuine and unconditional. His love never runs out; it is forever. God is always close, so tell Him what's on your mind.

PRAYER

God, You know me. You know everything about me, everything I am, everything I will be and everything I need. Help me to trust all that You are so I can and will come to You with everything, straight up, with no filters.

I want to remember and work on ......

I heard God say ......

ALL POWERFUL

*O Sovereign LORD! You made the heavens and earth by your strong hand
and powerful arm. Nothing is too hard for you!*
Jeremiah 32:17 NLT

God has complete and total power over everything, the big and the small. God has the power to do anything and everything He wants. This means He is self-sufficient and is God all by Himself. There is nothing He cannot do, so you can go to Him with everything you need. God's power is immense, complex, and supernatural.

When God spoke, the earth and everything in it came into being. When He raised Jesus from the dead, He gave Him a beating heart, breath in His lungs, and an eternal body; now, that's power!

You don't have to beg, borrow, steal, or compete with anyone to be all God called you to be. He chose you! God's power, activated by your faith (that means you must trust Him) gives you the strength to carry out the plans and purpose He has for you.

PRAYER

God, there is nothing you can't handle. I am going to stop trying to figure it out and let You work it out. I am putting everything in Your hands, so I know that Your hands are in everything. Thank You in advance for all you do to and through me.

GOD IS

I want to remember and work on ......

I heard God say ......

ALWAYS PRESENT

Is there any place I can go to avoid your Spirit? To be out of your sight? If I climb to the sky, you're there! If I go underground, you're there! If I flew on morning's wings to the far western horizon, you'd find me in a minute - you're already there waiting!
Psalm 139:7-10 MSG

When you are lonely and want or need help, you don't need to go to social media, make a call or text a friend. God is the source and has an answer for everything you need. He is available 24 hours a day, 7 days a week, 365 days a year. He never leaves you, He never turns His back on you and His doors are always open. He knows your life story from beginning to end. He knows what you've been through, what you are going through, and what challenges are headed your way.

God knows the right people who can help and the right doors to open to get you headed in the right direction. Trust every situation to the one that works everything out for your good, even the bad stuff. God told Jeremiah in 23:24 (NLT), *"Can anyone hide from me in a secret place? Am I not everywhere in all the heavens and earth."* There is no place you are that God is not. Trust Him to answer every question, every need.

PRAYER

God, thank You for always being around. Let me always feel Your presence and confidently walk out each day, each moment, and each breath without fear knowing that I am never alone.

I want to remember and work on ......

I heard God say ......

THE CREATOR

In the beginning, God created the heavens and the earth.
Genesis 1:1 NIV

God created the heavens and the earth, all that is seen and unseen. He created the skies, land, and sea, the sun, moon, and stars, as well as the fish, birds, and animals. On the 6th day, God created man and woman in His image. God created everything, including you. You are His original God design, a God shaped masterpiece, and His original authentic handiwork. God took His time and supernatural skills to create you just right.

Not only did God make you a work of art, but He threw away the mold when He was finished. God only makes one of one; He makes no copies. Even identical twins do not have the same fingerprints. There is nobody on this earth, just like you, that can do what you can do, exactly how you do it. No copying or comparing allowed. God created you special, with a holy purpose, in His image to do wonderful things.

PRAYER

God there is nothing and no one greater than You. You are the beginning and the end. You created the heavens, the earth, the moon, and the stars and everything You created is good. Lord, please help me know You and trust You as the intentional, powerful creator and source of everything, including me.

GOD IS

I want to remember and work on ......

I heard God say ......

FATHER

One God and Father of all, who is above all, and through all, and in you all.
Ephesians 4:6 KJV

S ometimes, I wish I could get some good advice or a hug from my dad, but he passed away 25 years ago. No matter where your dad is or is not, you have a father who loves you and knows everything about you. God's love never fails. He is available 24 hours a day, every day without needing a break or taking a vacation. The Bible says in *2 Corinthians 6:18 (ESV), "I will be a father to you, and you shall be sons and daughters to me, says the Lord Almighty."*

God is a loving father, and He cannot and does not lie. So, if He said it, trust me, He will do it. He has the resources to do what He says, so He says what He means. Guess what? God has no favorites. He doesn't love some and hate others or love some more than others. God loves and cares for all His children.

God loved you so much that He knew you would not learn how to live just by hearing or reading bible stories, so He sent His Son Jesus, the visible image, a perfect example of our invisible God, to show you what to do and how to do it. If that was not enough, He blessed you with His Holy Spirit gift. His gift is free. You do not pay for it or work to get it. He gave you His spirit free of charge to comfort, guide, and help you.

PRAYER

God help me know You as my eternal, supernatural Father, my dad, my safe place, the source of everything I could ever want or need. You gave me your best gifts, Jesus who died for me, and your Spirit who lives in me. Thank You for always sticking around.

I want to remember and work on ......

I heard God say ......

FORGIVING

The LORD is merciful and compassionate, very patient,
and full of faithful love.
Psalm 145:8 CEB

God finds no fault with us because every day is a fresh start with God. We get a do-over, a chance to talk with Him, to seek Him, to do what He says, and to go where He leads. God doesn't get angry, criticize, or lecture you. He won't get mad because you forgot what He said, failed to go where He sent you, or messed it up, so He had to give you a much-needed refresher course. I'm so glad God doesn't give bad online reviews and display all our faults for the world to see. God lovingly coaches us through each moment along our journey.

God knows transformation does not happen overnight, so he never gives up on you. I cannot tell you how often I had to ask God for forgiveness for being stingy, mean, or talking bad about someone, not going where He led, not trusting who He said I was, or not treating myself or others with love and compassion. God is always infinitely, unchangeably, unfailingly merciful, forgiving, loving, and kind.

PRAYER

Lord, thank you for hearing my cries, letting me unload my baggage, never telling me I told you so no matter how many times I come to You, and for always being my safe and happy place.

I want to remember and work on ......

I heard God say ......

GENEROUS

If you don't know what you're doing, pray to the Father. He loves to help. You'll get his help and won't be condescended to when you ask for it. Ask boldly, believingly, without a second thought.
James 1:5 CEB

God gives cheerfully, kindly, abundantly, plentifully, and lavishly. God's not stingy like many of us. He gives above and beyond what is asked, requested, or expected. He loves to help, and if you take inventory of your life, you will see many times where God provided just what you needed and more. Just in case you can't think of any of the great God gifts, think about this:

- He gave you life and created you beautifully.

- He gave you His Son Jesus and made you a joint heir.

- He gave you His Spirit to teach, guide, direct, comfort, and help you.

- He gives you a daily gift of grace, a clean slate, a do-over.

God's love and kindness never run out. You get it over and over and over again with unlimited eternal rights and privileges.

PRAYER

God, when I need You most, You never turn Your back on me. You are before and behind me. You always surround me with love and generosity. Thank You so much for always going above and beyond my expectations even when I'm not always generous to myself or anyone else.

I want to remember and work on ......

I heard God say

GOOD

O, taste and see that the Lord is good.
Psalm 34:8 NLV

God is inherently and perfectly good, and everything God does is good. It seems easier to believe in God's goodness when life is going as you planned, when you are healthy, happy, and living your best life. But even when troubles come your way, God is still good. Although you can't see how God is working it out, trust that he has a solution that will bless you in the end Romans 8:28 (NIV), says *"That in all things God works for the good of those who love him, who have been called according to his purpose." You might not feel or see the good right now, but it's coming.*

Early in my career, I had a co-worker who I thought was a friend. We used to have lunch and hang out sometimes until I found out she was talking negatively about me behind my back to our boss and coworkers. I thought nothing good could ever come from someone lying on you, killing your character, and possibly putting your job in jeopardy. But when I look back at that situation, the hurt of it all made me seek God, ask Him questions, read His word, and intently listen for His response. Even though being harmfully talked about did not feel good and I saw no good that could possibly from it at the time, it really did work out for my good. That situation helped me grow in faith. I learned to turn over the situation to Him and find peace with His outcome. I also found out who were truly my friends and made some new friends in the process.

PRAYER

God of goodness and mercy, You are the source of everything good. You are the source of everything I could ever want, need, dream, or imagine that is good for me and good to me. Thank you for Your never-ending goodness and kindness.

I want to remember and work on ......

I heard God say ......

HOLY

Holy, holy, holy is the Lord God Almighty, who was and is and is to come!
Revelation 4:8 ESV

The Merriam-Webster dictionary defines holiness as "exalted or worthy of complete devotion as one perfect in goodness and righteousness." To add to that definition, God is sacred, set apart, the beginning and the end, unlike anything that ever was or anything that will ever be in the future. He is not only perfect, but utterly perfect, complete, infinite, divine, and eternal.

These words are just our human expressions to try to wrap our minds around all that God is. The vastness, completeness, uniqueness, and all-encompassing, eternal, infinite, blemish-free, powerful source of all life that is God. There are really no words big enough, good enough, or in existence that can express all of whom and what God is. God just is! He is all that and then some! Infinite perfection, the one and only, the Great I Am, Alpha, Omega, Almighty, Master, Lord, Most High, Creator, Redeemer, Holy One and Father just to name a few. I'm sure you can add a few more to this list.

PRAYER

God thank you for revealing Yourself to me; You did not have to do it. I am humbled and honored to be yours and I pray each day I get to truly understand Your unlimited, supernatural, eternal greatness and power.

GOD IS

I want to remember and work on ......

I heard God say ......

LOVE

Anyone who does not love does not know God, for God is love.
1 John4:8 ESV

God is love. He is the embodiment, personification, and source of love. He loves completely, totally, and forever. Anything he creates or does is out of love because love is who He is. You might not always know what He is up to, how He's working on your behalf, what He will do next, or when He'll give you what you asked because if you did, He wouldn't be God. But because He loves you, you don't have to worry; your situation is being handled.

God is not fickle; He does not take back His love, His gifts, or His promises. You cannot be bad enough or messy enough for God to stop loving you. He just keeps on loving you through whatever you are going through. His love is consistent and everlasting.

When I was at my lowest, I did not feel loved or lovable. I lost my job, lost some friends and was going through a divorce all at the same time, but God loved me through it. Everything God does to you, for you, or through you is because of His love, period.

PRAYER

God, You simply love me. Help me to really, really, really know You are love, that You love me unconditionally, and no matter what happens, You will never stop loving me. Even when I don't get it right, help me to not feel guilty or beat myself up. Help me rest knowing Your love works everything out, even the bad stuff for my good.

I want to remember and work on ......

I heard God say ......

A MIRACLE WORKER

But if I were you, I would appeal to God; I would lay my cause before him.
He performs wonders that cannot be fathomed,
miracles that cannot be counted.
Job 5:8-9 NIV

God is always up to something good. He has done so many miracles, too many for me to count. He parted the Red Sea, saved three boys from burning in a fiery furnace, fed thousands with a few loaves of bread and some fish, and gave us Jesus, the savior. Although God did these things thousands of years ago, He is still working miracles.

Your being alive today reading this devotion is a miracle, every breath is a miracle, every heartbeat is a miracle, your organs working together in harmony is a miracle, and the daily rising and setting of the sun is a miracle. Miracles on miracles on miracles are happening every second of every day.

You might not always be focused on the miracles of God because life can often be overwhelming, but God is real, never late, and bigger than any situation you are facing. Trust Him to do a miracle. He did it before, and He can do it again.

PRAYER

Lord, in your power, do what only You can do. I am giving You all my worries, knowing You have the power to do miracles. Let me rest in Your heavenly peace as I take my hands off the situation.

I want to remember and work on ......

I heard God say ......

PATIENT

The Lord is not slow in keeping his promise, as some understand slowness.
He is patient with you.
2 Peter 3:9 NIV

God's patience and love for you never ends. I remember when God gave me the vision of going deeper in my spiritual growth journey by attending seminary. I did not immediately begin to research schools or programs. Nope, instead of moving forward where God was leading, I started asking people what they thought. I asked if they thought it was a good move, if they could see me as a minister, or if it was worth the time, effort, or money. Even in my unbelief, God did not give up on me.

Have you ever seen a baby trying to walk? When they stumble, they are encouraged to get back up and try again. They are reassured with statements like, you are doing so well, you almost got it or come on let's try again. You never hear anyone say get back up, dummy. I knew you couldn't do it, or you'll never get it right. Just like people coach the babies they love, to move forward and keep trying; God does the same with you. He never gives up on you, no matter how long it takes.

PRAYER

God, life has not always been easy and sometimes it just feels painful and confusing. When I feel uneasy, hurt, or alone please let me hear Your voice and feel your love, support, encouragement, and goodness overflow. I am not going to lean on my own understanding. Thank You for not rushing me and always lovingly waiting on me.

I want to remember and work on ......

I heard God say ......

PEACE

May the Lord of peace himself give you peace at all times and in every way.
2 Thessalonians 3:16 NIV

I f you look at the news, scroll through social media, or focus on the increased costs of gas, food, and housing, you will feel stressed the heck out. If you feel or surrender to the pressure to conform, be rich, beautiful, fit, and live lavishly, you might find yourself working nonstop with little time or space to breathe. Being stressed or overwhelmed with the trials of everyday life can be tough, but God is your place of peace, comfort, and rest.

Psalm 29:11 says, *"The Lord gives strength to his people and the Lord blesses his people with peace."* 1 Peter 5:7 says for you to *"Cast all your anxiety on him because he cares for you."* In Matthew 11:28, you are told, *"Come to me, all who are weary and burdened, and I will give you rest."*

All you need to do is trust God and give Him all your worries, issues, concerns, hurts, or questions, and He will give you peace. You can rest not because you have it all figured out but because you know God is working it out.

PRAYER

God, I am coming to You with my deepest fears, even the ones I am unwilling to talk about or acknowledge. You know everything and have the solution for all my troubles. Thank You for granting me your peace no matter where I am or what is going on.

I want to remember and work on ......

I heard God say ......

SOURCE

Everything I hope for comes from Him.
Psalm 62:5 MSG

A re you in need of something? Whatever it is, ask God for it because everything you want, need, or desire comes from Him. Tune in, plug in, tap into God, and let yourself and everyone else off the hook. Nobody can satisfy your wants and needs like God can. God knows the beginning, middle, and end of your story. Our answers, resources, and solutions are insufficient, but God's are divine, supernatural, infinite, and unlimited.

Rest and enjoy the peace of knowing that nothing is too big or too hard for God. He has the answer to all your needs, worries or problems so give Him your requests and keep your eyes, ears, and heart open for His help. He might use some unconventional methods or some people you would never expect but trust Him anyway. Ephesians 3:20 (MSG) says, "*God can do far more than you could ever imagine or guess or request in your wildest dreams.*" So, make your requests to God, knowing He hears you and has unlimited resources at His disposal.

PRAYER

God, You are all-powerful, all-knowing, and always present. You support me with never ending and unfailing love. You are always patient with me and always available to hear from me. You let me talk to you about everything. Your resources are endless and go beyond my wildest dreams. I trust You, no matter what.

I want to remember and work on ......

I heard God say ......

THE SAFE PLACE

God is our refuge and strength, always ready
to help in times of trouble.
Psalm 46:1 NLT

When I was little, I was afraid of storms, thunder, and lightning. During a storm, my family would turn off the lights and any appliances, then sit silently until the storm ended. However, if I was out, away from home and away from my parents during a storm, I felt unprotected, uncovered, and often afraid.

You never have to feel alone or unsafe with God. God is always ready, willing, and able to help. Whether you are dealing with physical, mental, emotional, relationship, career, or financial issues, God can handle your circumstances. Pray, talk to Him, tell Him what is going on, and ask for His help. He has the supernatural wisdom and strength to assist you, and while He is working it out, He's your safe place to wait it out.

PRAYER

Lord, I am not always the best at telling You I need help but thank You for not leaving me on my own to struggle or figure it out. Thanks for always being my breath of fresh air and the most comfortable place to dwell which gives me peace when my joy seems to be running on empty.

I want to rememb

GOD IS

er and work on ......

I heard God say ......

SOVEREIGN

Yours, O LORD, is the greatness and the power and the glory, and the victory, and the majesty, for all that is in the heavens and in the earth is yours. Yours is the kingdom, O LORD, and you are exalted as head above all.
1 Chronicles 29:11 ESV

Just in case you didn't know or thought God needed your help in being God, he doesn't. The dictionary defines sovereign as having the highest power or being completely independent. I like how the MSG puts it in Job 12:13-16 which says, *"True wisdom and real power belong to God; from him we learn how to live, and also what to live for."*

God has the absolute power, wisdom, and authority to do what He wants, when He wants, how He wants, and through whom He wants. I laugh when people or the culture try to say what God can do or who He can do it through.

If God can use a bush, a fire, a donkey, a prostitute, a womanizer, a drunk and a murderer, then He can use you. God uses ordinary people to extraordinary things. The bible says in 2 Corinthians 12:9 (NLT), *"My grace is all you need. My power works best in weakness."*

God is still God, and He is still healing, still creating, still protecting, still guiding, still helping, still talking, and still creating, and still making ways out of no ways.

PRAYER

God, nothing is too hard for You. Please help me stop putting limits on what You can do to, through and for me. Let me always remember and trust Your resources are supernatural, eternal, and unlimited.

I want to remember and work on ......

I heard God say ......

A SUPERNATURAL PROVIDER

And this same God who takes care of me will supply all your needs from his glorious riches, which have been given to us in Christ Jesus.
Philippians 4:19 NLT

God provides you with everything you need, and before you call any one or do anything, you need to talk to God. I keep hearing people say, I've done everything I could do; all I can do now is pray. Asking God should not be your last resort; it should be your first step, your priority. You need to PRAY first or talk to God and listen for His response before you even pick up the phone or search online for an answer.

Ephesians 3:20 (MSG) says, *"God can do anything, you know far more than you could ever imagine or guess or request in your wildest dreams!"* God knows everything, and His answers go beyond your common senses.

At this stage in life, I am always telling people I don't want anything God doesn't want for me, and anything I ask God for in prayer, before I end the prayer, I include "this or something better." You should include it, too. Because God's best will always supernaturally surpass any solution you can ever come up with.

PRAYER

Lord, I trust You with everything, the good, the bad, the ups and the downs. I know no good thing will You withhold from me. I trust You when you give, and I trust You when you don't. I trust the doors You open and the ones You shut. You can do far more than anything I ever want, need, or dream. Thank You in advance for who You are, all You do and all You will do.

I want to remember and work on ......

I heard God say ......

TRUSTWORTHY

Let's keep a firm grip on the promises that keep us going.
He always keeps his word.
Hebrews 10:23 MSG

God can be completely trusted. He always has the right answer, so you can trust the answer he sends. I am always baffled when God sends help, and it is not accepted because it doesn't come how we thought it would or through whom we thought it would come. You thought the answer would come from a man, but God sent a woman. You thought the answer would come from someone experienced and esteemed, but God sent a young person, or you asked God for money, but he sent you to training.

God knows our end from our beginning, so trusting Him will never be in vain. He promised to supply all your needs according to His riches in glory, but you can't tell God how to be God. You must trust Him based on who He is, which is a divinely good, good father who knows everything, owns everything, is always present, and keeps His word. God hears your cries, so trust Him with the solution.

PRAYER

God, I know I often think I'm right and I don't always immediately trust,
I even panic at times but help me never doubt You know what's best for me.

GOD IS

You always show up. Even when You are quiet, I know You are working it all out for my good and that everything is will be all right.

I want to remember and work on ……

I heard God say ……

A WAYMAKER

No temptation has overtaken you that is not common to man. God is faithful, and he will not let you be tempted beyond your ability, but with the temptation he will also provide the way of escape, that you may be able to endure it.
1 Corinthians 10:13 NIV

Have you ever needed help really quickly, immediately, right now but had no idea where the help would come from? Well, God is the supreme way-maker. He makes ways where there seems to be no way.

I once had a gift card I carried around for 8 months. Each time I said I was going to use it; I forgot or left it at home. One day, a lady was telling me she was having a rough time, homeless, and praying for help. I normally would not be at this store at this time, but as I listened, the Lord told me to give her the gift card. I thanked God and her for being so transparent. I am sure it wasn't easy to share her struggles with a stranger.

We both had tears in our eyes because I assured her our meeting was not just luck or happenstance but a divine appointment, an answer to prayer, a heavenly delay. I told her how long I had carried around the card in my purse, and how many opportunities I had but failed to use it but at the right time and the right place when she needed God most, He answered her prayers.

Our divine set up also answered my prayer because sometimes, when God is quiet, I will ask Him to speak to me and let me know he is still listening. During our interaction,

41

God spoke, I listened, and God blessed us both at the same time.

PRAYER

Heavenly Father, thank You for always listening and using all Your divine ways to do what is best for me. Let me always come to You first before I call anyone or seek help from anywhere else. Your solutions are endless, eternal, and infinite. You always have the best and right answer.

I want to remember and work on ......

I heard God say ......

WISE

Oh, the depth of the riches, both of the wisdom and knowledge of God! How unsearchable are His judgments and unfathomable His ways!
Romans 11:33 NLT

Wisdom is more than just head knowledge and intelligence. A truly wise person is someone who understands all the facts and makes the best decisions. A wise person uses heart, mind, and soul together with skill and competence before taking action.

If you have a question, need some answers, have a problem, don't know what to do or where to go, can't figure it out, need direction, protection, healing, peace, or increase, go to God, your source instead of calling Tyrone or checking the horoscopes. God, your Father, knows all about you. He knows what you need when you need it.

The answers God gives are real, genuine, honest, and true, and they are relevant, appropriate, important, and meaningful for your situation. What God gives you is always better than anything you can ever come up with. His answers are divine from His eternal perspective, beyond your common sense, and always right on time.

PRAYER

God, in my darkest times and at all times, You take care of me. My mind cannot fathom all that is available to You. You have unlimited resources and make ways where I can see no way. God there is nothing that escapes you. Give me the wisdom, strength, and confidence to make choices that please you. Thank You for giving me all that I need.

I want to remember and work on ......

I heard God say ......

PART II

I AM

You are beautiful. You are amazing. You are a perfect God design. There is nothing wrong with you or anyone else. It is not your job to fix anyone, and that includes you. There is nothing that you must do, must have, must be, or need to figure out.

You are a divine design with a God given purpose, and you are extraordinarily gifted with all the love, help, power, direction, protection, and resources needed to complete your God given assignment. You do not need to rush because God's assignment will unfold as you grow and master each step. So, base your truth, worth, path, and uniqueness on what God says about you so the miracle of all that you are never wavers.

Each time you read the title of the devotions in this chapter, put **"I am"** in front of it. If God said it, you can be certain of it.

BLESSED

And my God will meet all your needs according to the riches
of his glory in Christ Jesus.
Philippians 4:19 NIV

Blessed means you have the favor of God. I like the song by Norman Hutchins, "God's Got a Blessing," in which he sings, "God's got a blessing with your name on it." Not only does God have blessings for you, but He's already blessed you tremendously with breath in your lungs, with God's word to guide you, Jesus, as your savior, and the Holy Spirit inside you with all the power you need to see you through anything.

If that was not enough, God gives you eternal promises of blessings like in Luke 6:38 (CEV), *"If you give to others, you will be given a full amount in return. It will be packed down, shaken together, and spilling over into your lap"*, or Philippians 4:19 (NIV), *"And my God will supply all your needs according to His riches in glory in Christ Jesus."*

God has blessings, on top of blessings, on top of blessings. He is rich and abundant in everything good and those who believe in Him are truly blessed.

PRAYER

Gracious wonderful and awesome God, thank you for everything You are, everything You do and everything You will do. Thank You for giving me your best and blessing me in ways I could never ever imagine. Give me the vision to let my life unfold in ways that are beyond my wildest dreams and let me always go where You need me most.

I want to remember and work on ......

I heard God say ......

CHOSEN

But you are the ones chosen by God, chosen for the high calling of priestly work, chosen to be a holy people, God's instruments to do his work and speak out for him, to tell others of the night and-day difference he made for you from nothing to something, from rejected to accepted.
1 Peter 2:9 MSG

You are chosen to do wonderful and important things. I remember when I started preaching and teaching, people told me I did not look like a minister. I did not fit the perception of what a minister should look like, talk like, or dress like. To be honest, I even questioned why God chose me. Although skeptical, I prayed for my next steps and enrolled in seminary.

However, after I graduated and started ministering, I was so critical of myself. I picked apart my messages. I would criticize my clothes, my hair, my weight, and my posture. I was driving myself crazy! It seemed like I paid no attention to the good, like when people said the message spoke to them or how the teaching changed their perspective. Then I heard God say, you were chosen for this assignment so keep going where I lead you. God created and handpicked you, specifically for your assignment, too.

PRAYER

God, help me feel the fear and say yes, yes, and yes to my assignment anyway. With Your help I will not worry about other people's expectations and opinions or give into my many fears but with faith guide me confidently in the direction You send me.

I want to remember and work on ......

I heard God say ......

COMPLETE

Our God gives you everything you need, makes you everything you need to be.
2 Thessalonians 1:2 MSG

The Bible says you are God's workmanship, created to do good works God prepared in advance for you to do. God made you, and anything God makes is awesome! God is the source of everything you need. Your completeness is found in Him.

I used to have a neighbor that was always telling me about some party, some event, some activity I missed that was so fantastic. The descriptions were so hyped up that I really thought I should have been there. Until I started going to the events only to find out they were not particularly amazing or what I was told they would be. Social media is like those hyped-up events my neighbor used to talk about because the reels, pictures and posts have a way of making you feel left out of the party.

You see the beautiful faces, the amazing places, all the fun everyone is having and how great everyone looks that you can start to feel like you are missing life. However, those pictures are just a snapshot of time, and to be honest many of them are fake, enhanced or airbrushed to make them perfect. Trust me, you are not missing anything.

You see, God only makes one of anything, so do not compare yourself, your life, your activities, or your purpose because your DNA or the special stuff inside that makes you great is one of a kind. It cannot be recreated or duplicated. God's just super dope like that.

PRAYER

God You are everything to me. My Father, my maker, my guide, my peace, my provider, my protection, my savior, my strength, my purpose, my doctor, my advisor, my confidant, my truth, and my source. With You, I am complete, lacking and missing nothing.

I want to remember and work on ......

I heard God say ......

DESTINED FOR GREATNESS

Study this Book of Instruction continually. Meditate on it day and night so you will be sure to obey everything written in it. Only then will you prosper and succeed in all you do.
Joshua 1:8 NLT

God has given you everything you need to succeed. God is always leading you, guiding you, helping you as well as giving you instruction and wisdom for your journey. Whenever I forget God is rooting for me to succeed or has my back no matter what, I read this scripture. The word is very clear about what it takes to be successful, which is:

1. Keep God's word on your lips, talk about it, read it, google it, and ask questions about it. Spend time and energy on it.

2. Meditate on God's word day and night. Think deeply about what it says, reflect on it, and internalize it so it guides your actions.

3. Be careful to do what God's word says. We are to love God and love people; that includes loving you too.

You do not have to be great in your own strength; remember to ask God's Spirit, His Holy Spirit on the inside of you, to help you reach the goals and plans God has for you.

PRAYER

God, give me the sight to see what You see in me. Help me trust each part of the process. I am not going to lie, sometimes I am scared but teach me to live, be and do everything with excellence as if I am doing it all for You. Lord, let me hear Your voice louder than any others. Amen.

I want to remember and work on ......

I heard God say ......

A DIVINE DESIGN

God said, "Now we will make humans, and they will be like us. We will let them rule the fish, the birds, and all other living creatures."
Genesis 1:26 CEV

You are God's child, a masterpiece, a one-of-a-kind, God creation. God knew you, thought about you, and loved you even before you were born. There are no people God created by mistake and there is not one extra, unneeded person in the world.

You are not an afterthought, someone's pet project, or a second-class citizen. You were created special specifically by God, in the image of God, so you have the characteristics of God, which are love, joy, peace, patience, kindness, goodness, compassion, wisdom, self-control, gentleness, and faithfulness.

Not only are you God's child, the child of the Most High, but you are a joint heir with Christ. Being a joint heir with Christ means you get all the benefits of being God's child with unlimited access, which is in effect 24 hours a day, today, tomorrow, and forever.

PRAYER

Lord, help me to embrace my heir status by loving myself unconditionally, boldly stepping into all You have designed me to be, and trusting I always have access to You. Thank You for giving me Your best 100% of the time. I know the best is yet to come.

I want to remember and work on ......

I heard God say ......

FORGIVEN

Because of the sacrifice of the Messiah, his blood poured out on the altar of the Cross, we're a free people — free of penalties and punishments chalked up by all our misdeeds.
Ephesians 1:7 MSG

This is a great scripture, but I also like what Psalm 130:3 (NIV) says, *"If you, LORD, kept a record of sins, Lord, who could stand?"* Lord knows if God kept a record of each time I did not act in love, did not pray, put myself in compromising positions, did not tell the truth, was mean, told someone off, or did not act in a way that demonstrated Christ; I surely would not be able to stand! I would be lying on the floor crying, begging for forgiveness and a second chance.

God certainly does not keep records of your wrongs, how often you mess up, how many times you did not listen, let someone take advantage of you, or talked about the things you hated about yourself, your life, your body, where you live, or where you work. God keeps on loving and forgiving you even when you do not forgive yourself.

Do not let anyone, even you, hold you hostage about your past. No one is perfect, and God uses all people, flaws, and all. If anyone ever tries to bring you your past, tell them Jesus already paid the price.

PRAYER

God, I know that You know I am not perfect. I am a constant work in progress, but I am trying. Please do not give up on me. I am humbly thankful that each day You give me is a fresh start, a do-ever, another chance to stay on the course of my spiritual assignment. I am eternally grateful.

I want to remember and work on ......

I heard God say ......

FREE

Christ has set us free to live a free life. So, take your stand!
Never again let anyone put a harness of slavery on you.
Galatians 5:1 MSG

Anyone who knows me knows I do not always follow the so-called rules. My life, my thoughts, and my journey have often been unconventional, as I have done and tried things many people would not. I love the freedom to do me. From my love of education and learning to my natural hair and big earrings.

However, in this verse, Paul isn't just talking about worldly stuff, like how you dress, what you eat, or how you look. God is saying you are free to have a relationship with Him through Christ without asking anyone's permission and without needing a mediator, translator, special time, or place.

If you want to talk to God, then do that. If you want to pray, then do it. If you have questions, then ask them. You do not have to get your information second-hand or only at a specific time or place. You can go straight to God, your source of all things, without stopping for someone to give you directions or approval.

PRAYER

I am free, I am free, praise the Lord I am free. God thank You for letting me know I do not have to get preapproval from anybody to be all You created and called me to be. I do not have to walk, talk, or act like anyone else to be loved or accepted. I can bring me to life, just as You designed me. Thank you, thank you, thank you.

I want to remember and work on ......

I heard God say ......

GIFTED

God has also given each of us different gifts to use. If we can prophesy, we should do it according to the amount of faith we have.
Romans 12:6 CEV

Did you know you are gifted? Well, you are! God has given you gifts, talents, and abilities that can change the world. Although some people have the same gift, that gift will look different and be different when you bring it to life. I do not care what has happened in your past; the world needs YOU!

Remember, you do not have to do things the same way they have always been done, copy someone's style, take the familiar route, or stay in your comfort zone. You were created and designed to do more than the basics of waking up, eating, going to work, watching television, checking social media, sleeping, and then repeating.

The Holy Spirit specifically blessed you with precious gifts that should be discovered, uncovered, embraced, and used. Your gifts are not just for you but for you to share with the world so that as you do you, people can see God.

PRAYER

Gracious God, please help me know, understand, appreciate, and unapologetically use the gifts You have given me. God, I trust you so use me.

61

Speak through me, think through me, create through me. Let what You put in me shine so much that people see You, want to know and love You too.

I want to remember and work on ......

I heard God say ......

GOOD

We have everything we need to live a life that pleases God. It was all given to us by God's own power, when we learned he had invited us to share in his wonderful goodness.
2 Peter 1:3 CEV

Good means no matter what's going on or what it looks like, you're all right, and everything that's happening is working out in your favor. I was the speaker at an event, and my book **I Look Good, I Feel Good, I Am Good** had just come out. I had t-shirts printed with the title to encourage women that no matter what is happening, God's got it.

A lady said, "I could never wear a shirt that says that because I am not always a good person and I make mistakes." Just so you know, saying you are good does not mean you will not experience problems or always make the best choices. Saying you are good means even though you don't always do the right thing, say the right thing or bad things happen, you're okay. If you are not ok right at this moment, then your ok is coming. It is like what it says in Psalm 23:1 (NIV), "*The Lord is my shepherd,* I lack NOTHING," period.

PRAYER

God, can You please help me remember there is nothing You cannot handle. I can't solve my issues so today and every day I turn it all over to You. I am feeling, speaking, and living like the best is already here, and it is. I am focusing on all good stuff. You got it and You got me, so it is all good.

I want to remember and work on ......

I heard God say ......

HEALED

This is the confidence we have in approaching God: that if we ask anything according to his will, he hears us. And if we know that he hears us—whatever we ask—we know that we have what we asked of him.
1 John 14-15 NIV

As the seasoned saints say, keep on living because, at some point, you will have something that hurts. We ask for physical healing for our bodies, but mental, emotional, and spiritual healing are just as important. You might need to be healed from past hurts like family trauma, childhood abuse, or bullying and the resulting effects of low self-esteem or diminished self-worth. You could need healing from self-sabotaging behaviors like overeating, overspending, drinking too much, watching too much television, or spending too much time on social media.

You could need to be healed from the need to please, from the need to always be right, or the need to control people, situations, and your environment. We all need to be healed from something. Ask God to heal your issue no matter what it is. God has the supernatural, wonder-working, miracle power to heal it!! God says you can call those things that are not as if they are, so speak a healing over you. Let the weak say I am strong, let the sick say I am well, let the broke say I am rich.

PRAYER

God, you know everything and just the right prescription for what ails me. Thank You in advance for keeping me in my right mind and in perfect peace even when I can't see what You are doing to fix it. Thank you for my complete and total supernatural healing that only comes through you.

I want to remember and work on ......

I heard God say ......

LOVED

For God so loved the world, that he gave his only Son, that whoever believes in him should not perish but have eternal life.
John 3:16 NIV

When I think of this scripture, it says God so loved the world, and that whoever believes in Christ will have eternal life, and that whoever includes you. "Whoever" is inclusive; it does not include conditions like only rich people, only people with degrees, only people from the right side of town.

God's love is unconditional. It doesn't matter what you have done or what you will do; if you are broke, homeless, depressed, or didn't finish school, God loves you. His love never runs out, and because of His love, He never gives up on you.

I like what Paul tells the Romans in 8:38, (MSG), *"I'm absolutely convinced that nothing, nothing living or dead, angelic or demonic, today or tomorrow, high or low, thinkable or unthinkable—absolutely nothing can get between us and God's love because of the way that Jesus our Master has embraced us."* I am absolutely convinced, too; nothing can or will separate you from the love of God!!

PRAYER

God, I want to be the person you created me to be so please help me never forget no matter what happens, I am absolutely, infinitely loved. There is no place where You cannot find me, there is nothing I can do to turn off Your love. Your love goes beyond anything I can ever understand, and I thank You for allowing me to experience Your love every day of my life.

I want to remember and work on ......

I heard God say ......

NEVER ALONE

I'm convinced that nothing can separate us from God's love in Christ Jesus our Lord: not death or life, not angels or rulers, not present things, or future things, not powers or height or depth, or any other thing that is created.
Romans 8:38-39 NIV

We moved to Florida when I was 7 months pregnant, without a doctor and a permanent place to live. My husband drove an hour each way to work while I worked virtually. The maximum length of time we could stay at the property we rented was 4 weeks, but I knew we would probably need about 7 weeks before securing a permanent housing solution. Leaving our home in Washington, D.C., was a test of our faith because we were going where God led even though we could not see the next steps.

Every day, we talked to God about our situation and our needs. He sent me to the front desk of our rental at the right time to talk to just the right person who could extend our stay, and he gave us peace as we waited, so we weren't stressed out as He worked it out. He led us to an OB/GYN doctor and eventually, we found a home and my son was born a week later.

Don't let fear stop you. Have faith that God is always open and available to hear from you. His doors are always open!

PRAYER

God, I might not always be 100% sure of what I'm doing, but I trust You are always 100% with me, ready and willing to help. Just because I don't always feel Your presence does not mean You are gone. Thank You for never abandoning me. You never give up, you never give up, you never give up.

I want to remember and work on ......

I heard God say ......

POWERFUL

I can do all things through Christ who gives me strength.
Philippians 4:13 NLT

The power in you comes from God, and His power is unlimited. You can do whatever you need to do in life, whatever God has sent you to do because you have the full backing and power of God. When you feel like you can't, ask God to give you the strength so you can.

A lady once asked me, "How do you get up in front of people and speak?" I told her, "I'd be lying if I said I was always comfortable speaking in front of crowds. But before I speak, I ask God to talk, so I say what He wants said the way He wants me to say it." God is the source of your help and your strength. If He sent you to it, He will get you through it.

I love to hear stories of God's strength at work in people. Like the 10-year-old twins who said they felt the power of Jesus helping them as they saved their dad from drowning, the father who was able to lift a car that fell on his child, or the man who donated 20 million dollars to the college he could not afford to attend. The next time you are faced with an impossible situation, remember Ephesians 1:19, "*With God all things are possible.*"

PRAYER

Lord, let Your Holy Spirit move through me and give me the strength, courage, wisdom, confidence, direction, and protection to accomplish everything you created me to do. God refresh, renew, revive, and restore me so I can complete my assignments. Thank you so much, Amen.

I want to remember and work on ......

I heard God say ......

PROTECTED

The Lord keeps you from harm and watches over your life. The Lord keeps watch over you as you come and go, both now and forever.
Psalm 121:7-8 NLT

Everyone wants to feel safe, so we look to people and devices to protect our homes, money, health, and relationships. God protects you from anything, and everything meant to harm you, including seen and unseen dangers. He watches over you and your family. He provides shelter in times of trouble. He prevents attacks from the enemy, and even when the attacks come, He will use them for your good. God is so good that He eternally protects your purpose so no one will rob you of it or take your place.

I thank God for His protection. He protected me when I was in trouble, when I didn't know I needed protection, and even when I did not listen to His promptings to stop, turn right, wait, or go in another direction. John 10:28 (NGV) says, *"I go to bed and sleep in peace, because Lord, only you keep me safe."*

PRAYER

God, I have been in some scary and some messy situations. There is nothing I am facing You don't know about. Thank You for keeping me close to you and giving me access to Your limitless, unwavering eternal protection. Things might not always look like what I want, but I know with Your protection in place, it's everything I need.

YOU ARE

I want to remember and work on ......

I heard God say ......

QUALIFIED

God has given each of you a gift from his great variety of spiritual gifts.
Use them well to serve one another.
1 Peter 4:10-11 NIV

God created you in advance to do something great, and He gave you the gifts, talents, skills, and abilities to get it done. You are officially certified, designated, and created to do what God intended. As they say, "What God has for you, no devil in hell can take away." God does not take back His gifts when we mess up, don't measure up or don't use them perfectly. You have God's seal of approval, and your assignment is for life; it does not expire.

Do you know your assignment? If you don't; ask God, what do you want me to do with my life? Another great way to find out your assignment is to ask yourself, "When am I happiest?" Then write down the answer(s). You'll often find your assignment is most likely something you really love to do and will do even without thinking about it.

Your assignment will unfold over time. As you master one step, then the next step is ready for your attention. You have what you need, and you're on the right track. Anointed, appointed, selected, equipped, guided, and protected that's what you are.

PRAYER

Amazing God, I trust every step of my life to you. I believe the gifts You put inside me were specifically designed for my assignments. Develop me as I listen to Your voice and direct me down the paths You choose. I know the path that leads to You is what I need most. Keep me going in the right direction so I end up where I am supposed to be.

I want to remember and work on ......

I heard God say ......

VALUABLE

For we are God's handiwork, created in Christ Jesus to do good works, which
God prepared in advance for us to do.
Ephesians 2:10 NIV

God made you special and unique, beautiful, and a special edition, so there's no need to compare yourself to anyone. God does not make copies or imitations. He only makes one of anything; even if it looks the same, it's not. We often complain about things we don't like about ourselves. We compare our looks, our bodies, our lives, our careers, or our bank accounts, which can feel like we must strive to be more, have more, or do more.

Tune out the inner and outside critics as well as the unsolicited opinions because what makes you different makes you beautiful. You are one of one, a masterpiece, a work of God's genius and there will never be another exactly like you who can do what you do the way that only you can do it. What God put in you is greater and more valuable than any negative thought or perceived limitation.

PRAYER

God, you take care of my every need. Help me remember I am an original
God design, wanted and eternally cared for by You. Help me to focus on
what's good and have an attitude of gratitude for each moment and every

breath You give. Let the gifts of love, joy, peace, patience, kindness, gentleness, and self-control be evident in everything I think, say, and do.

I want to remember and work on ......

I heard God say ......

VICTORIOUS

No, in all these things we are more than conquerors
through him who loved us.
Romans 8:37 NIV

I love the movie "The Matrix" because the main character, Neo, had to make a choice either to live like the culture and do what everybody else was doing or take the narrow road, the road that leads to a life of Godly purpose. He had the answers within himself all along, but he failed to act on that information. He was comfortable, complacent, and stuck on autopilot (does this sound familiar?)

In the beginning, Neo did not trust what God told him, that he was strong, there for a reason, with a purpose to do great things. Neo was constantly seeking validation from others and running in fear of his opposition, Mr. Smith, who wanted him to stay asleep to his purpose and his greatness. But one day, Neo got tired of running and finally stood still to hear the still, small voice of God.

God's unrelenting encouragement helped him stand firm and fight back against Mr. Smith and his accomplices, their disdain, and all their oncoming bullets. Their attacks could no longer stop Neo from becoming who God destined him to be. In the end, Neo believed what God said about him that he was strong, powerful, and destined to change the world for the better. He believed with all his heart and began to fight back. He knew no weapon formed against him would ever prosper, and NO weapon formed against you will ever prosper either.

PRAYER

God, thank You for letting me know I am not here to beat anyone at anything. Although I don't always feel victorious, thank You for fighting for me and giving me victory in ways that are right to You. From this point on, I don't want anything You don't won't for me. Amen

I want to remember and work on ......

I heard God say ......

WANTED

Are you tired? Worn out? Burned out on religion? Come to me. Get away with me and you'll recover your life. I'll show you how to take a real rest.
Matthew 11:28 MSG

We seem to always have an excuse about why we want to wait before we come to God with our needs, our hurts, and our desires. For some reason, we think we must clean up our lives and have everything picture perfect before we talk to God. It's not the right time. When I get married or when I have children then I will come to you. When I'm older or when I get myself together then it will be the right time.

God says come as you are. He said this long before it was a popular reference to the dress code. You don't have to pull yourself together to talk to God. He will listen even with tears running down your face or snot coming out your nose, broke, busted, disgusted, frustrated, drug addicted, jobless, homeless, overweight, malnourished, bald, or with a bad wig. He will you're your cries, no special attire needed.

God takes you just as you are, and He will give you the rest you need, the peace you need, the love you need, and the direction you need. Give your worries to God. Although they may not disappear immediately, you can let go so you no longer have to do the heavy lifting.

PRAYER

Thank You, God, for choosing me, for choosing to love me, and for choosing to always care for me. Teach me to know I am not here by accident, and neither is anyone else. I may not always feel loved or confident but show me how to love and forgive like You.

I want to remember and work on ......

I heard God say ......

A WORK IN PROGRESS

And I am certain that God, who began the good work within you,
will continue his work until it is finally finished on the day
when Christ Jesus returns.
Philippians 1:6 NLT

To tell the truth, sometimes I'm afraid of who God says I am. When I pray, I don't always trust God can answer quickly, so I listen to the voices that say, "You can't do that, you're too old, nobody has done that before, or if it isn't broke, don't fix it." If you are like me, you might even beat yourself up for not moving forward immediately or for wasting time with people who don't have your best interests at heart.

It's okay if you don't always get it right the first time; life is a process. The beauty of your life is that your it does not happen overnight it's a sweet God designed journey of unfolding with twists and turns that always turn out for your good. There are things you must learn and areas where you need to grow so give yourself time, permission, and space to look for God in everything.

Imagine if a woman became pregnant today and gave birth to a 150-pound baby the next day; that would be very confusing to everyone involved and most likely extremely painful to the woman giving birth. God knows everything you need to complete your assignment, so give you a break, show you some grace, dial down the stress levels and trust God's timing. He makes everything perfect in its own time.

PRAYER

Oh, Heavenly Father God, help me not focus on the past or what I think didn't work out. Let me stop feeling guilty and beating myself up. I believe everything that happens helps me know and love You more. I am ready to forgive everyone, including myself, and keep it moving. I am bringing all my concerns to you as I trust your timing, because it is most certainly perfect, just like You.

I want to remember and work on ......

I heard God say ......

WORTHY

Even the hairs on your head are all counted. Don't be afraid.
You are worth more than many sparrows.
Luke 12:7 CEB

God loves you, and He took His time creating you because you are fearfully and wonderfully made. Since everything God makes is good, that includes you, you are worthy of all God wants and has for you. I often see people doing the most to prove their worth, to be liked or accepted. Sadly, as soon as they reach the standard or meet the requirements, the standard and the requirements change. There is more you must do; more you must be or more you must have. It's like you're running around in circles trying to get to the top, but you never measure up.

Thank God he does not put up a list of requirements we must meet or exceed to be loved by Him. Your life is a gift given by God, your heavenly Father, and His love is free. You don't have to be performing Patty or Peter perfect to be worthy of it. You do not get an A for pretending to be something or someone you are not or beating yourself up for any mistakes you've made along the way. God knows all about you, and He loves, cares, and values you anyway.

PRAYER

God, I know I may not always show appreciation of me, my mind, my body, my choices, or my life but help me understand and love me unconditionally like You love me.

I want to remember and work on ......

I heard God say ......

PART III

BE
ENCOURAGED

This is your life, the main event, the perfect time for you to take action. It's time to move forward trusting and knowing God has you covered even when it does not look or feel like it. Faith without works is dead. To put it another way, you can't just sit on the sidelines of your life, be a bystander and expect God to do all the work. You must do your part, invite God in then trust Him to do his part. Your part can be praying, reading, meditating, working towards the goal or taking some time to rest and enjoy what God has created.

You are worthy of all the things God has for you. Be proud of you and all the progress you have made, especially all the progress people cannot see. Use the encouragement in this section to help you successfully maneuver the twists and turns of your journey. Remember, you are allowed to be a masterpiece and a work in progress at the same time.

I'm rooting for you to be your best self, God's child, fearfully and wonderfully made, the absolutely amazing person God created you to be!

ASK GOD FOR WHAT YOU WANT AND NEED

Keep on asking, and you will receive what you ask for. Keep on seeking, and you will find. Keep on knocking, and the door will be opened to you.
Matthew 7:7 NLT

I have been in situations where I expected someone to help me because I helped them. Whatever they needed, I was there, but it seemed like when I was in need, they were nowhere to be found. But that's okay because God is the source of everything you want, need, or desire. Not your friends, not your job, and not your significant other. You don't have yet because you don't ask God. Go to God with all your requests and trust Him to provide, but when you ask, believe you will receive it or something better.

I always like to include the something better part at the end of my request because God knows everything, and your ask might not be big enough or might not be right for you. You can trust God to always give you His best in His time, so add the "or better" at the end and watch Him do greater things than you ever thought possible.

PRAYER

God, I trust You with my wants and needs. Help me to keep it moving in peace, patience, and joy as You work everything out as you see fit in your timing.

89

ENCOURAGEMENT

I want to remember and work on ......

I heard God say ......

BE IT, DO IT, LIVE IT

Keep this Book of the Law always on your lips; meditate on it day and night
so that you may be careful to do everything written in it.
Then you will be prosperous and successful.
Joshua 1:8 NIV

God knows everything. He knows what you want, what you need, where you're going, your fears, your hopes, and your dreams. God has a reason, a purpose, and a plan for your life. It's the reason you're alive and have breath in your body. You don't have to figure it out by yourself; God's word is the roadmap, the GPS, and the way to get you where He wants and needs you to be.

God's word is here for you to read, listen to, love, share, use, and master. God is not looking for people who have memorized the Bible and can recite all the books backward and forward. James 1:22 (NIV) says, *"Do what the word says, or you are only fooling yourselves and talking words."* God knows you are a work in progress, so He is not looking for perfection but those who are willing to allow Him to lead the way, so they look, and act more like Him.

Today is another chance to realize your life is important. Honor yourself and step into the greatness of God's grace while you enjoy the freedom of His truth to become your best you.

PRAYER

God, help me not just read or hear Your word but help me understand it. Lead me, guide me and make it come to life, so I fearlessly do what it says.

I want to remember and work on ......

I heard God say ......

BELIEVE

In my distress I called upon the LORD; to my God I cried for help. From his temple he heard my voice, and my cry to him reached his ears.
Psalm 18:6 ESV

God knows I have had some trying times in my life. I wrote about having my son at 40 years old, but what I left out was that the doctors said I was too old to conceive and carry to term a healthy baby, the culture said I was old, my eggs were old and that I would have an old looking baby. Some said my child would be embarrassed to have me show up at school because I would look like the grandmother instead of the mom.

What about the great grandmother that earned her college degree at the age of 100? I am sure that was not easy, and I bet she too had people who said negative things about her being too old to accomplish her goals too. Maybe you have a different story about something you wanted to be, do, or have and it seems like you were facing insurmountable odds.

Well, if you ever need help, if you feel like it's not working out, go to God with all your cries, believe He heard you and that he will help. God has already given you some promises to help in your unbelief like:

- God is with you. Psalm 23:4
- God can still the storm to a whisper. Psalm 107:28-29
- With God nothing is impossible. Matthew 19:26
- God will help you. Isaiah 41:13

- He has promised to sustain you. Psalm 55:22
- He promised to work it all out, no matter what you are going through for your good. Romans 8:28

PRAYER

Loving father God, you have promised to love, care, and help me. I really want to believe what you said, please help me in my unbelief. Give me the wisdom to do everything Your way.

I want to remember and work on ......

I heard God say ......

BE PLEASED WITH ALL OF YOU

So be content with who you are, and don't put on airs.
God's strong hand is on you; he'll promote you at the right time.
1 Peter 5:6 MSG

Do you ever get tired of people trying to tell you what to do, how to act, where to live, and how to be? Ads and commercials tell you that you are not good enough unless you take this pill, buy this product, lose weight, or have white teeth. The pressure never stops. To be successful, you must walk like this, talk like this, or dress like this. It's okay to be inspired by someone, but don't lose your mind trying to meet all the requirements of the culture or of your good-meaning family and friends.

You do not need anyone to approve of your looks, your clothes, your career, your calling, or your life. God has made you with gifts and talents that need to be shared with the world that no one can bring you to life like you can.

The moment you learn to love you, work what you've got, and stop trying to fit in because God is calling you to stand out is the moment, you'll realize you are truly a one-of-a-kind work of art with the full strength and power of God to help you do what needs to be done.

PRAYER

Lord, help me love and appreciate how You made me and the gifts You gave me. Let me no longer compare how You have designed me and what You have given me to what anyone else has. Let me love me and create what You want created with joy and gratitude.

I want to remember and work on ......

I heard God say ......

BE YOUR OWN CHEERLEADER

Kind words are like honey, sweet to the soul and healthy for the body.

Proverbs 16:24 NLT

We can be our worst critics. I recorded a short devotional and was excited to see the video, but when I played it, all I could think about was what I disliked. Instead of focusing on the positive words of the videographer who said, "I love our energy, or all the messages need to be this hype", I focused on my discontent. What you focus on grows, so focus on encouraging you and make time to celebrate your wins.

Do you need a boost of confidence? Affirmations are a great way to remind yourself of the promises of God. Here are a few encouraging statements to get you started: I am loved, I am strong, I am beautiful, I am powerful, I am happy, I am blessed, I am chosen, I am worthy, I am God's masterpiece, I am always supported, I am one of a kind, I am on the right track, I am valuable, I am wanted, I am healthy, I am well, I am good, I am awesome!! Add some of your own to this list and repeat them to yourself first thing in the morning and before you go to sleep until you really believe what you say.

PRAYER

Dear God, please develop my sight so I see myself as You see me, which is chosen, loved, gifted, anointed, appointed, and supported to do great things.

I want to remember and work on ......

I heard God say ......

CHANGE HOW YOU LOOK AT THINGS

I pray that God, the source of hope, will fill you completely with joy and peace because you trust in him.
Romans 15:13 NLT

When my son entered high school the school start and end times were very different than the middle school hours. My son had to be at school an hour and a half earlier than the previous year. We had to wake up around 5:45 to leave the house by 6:30 to make it through traffic and get to school on time. That was an adjustment. Mody mind and body felt like it should still be asleep under the covers, in bed.

I had a strong dislike and day I say disdain for these life adjustments. My mood and my attitude were not very joyful, or peace filled. I felt myself complaining when I had to get up, get him up and drive through traffic. One day I got tired of complaining because it was making me unhappy, making my son unhappy and I did not want to ride to school for the entire school year with a bad attitude. So, I began to ask God what I could learn from getting up early and how I could use the earlier wake up time to spend more time with Him.

Just that change of thought about my situation took me from discomfort and complaining to thankful and blessed. As I thought about God's grace it changed my energy and attitude. I began to thank God for the blessing of having a place to sleep, a car to drive, time with my son and eyes to see the beauty of God's sunrise each day after I dropped him off on the drive home.

Are there some things you dislike that you could look at in a new and different way? When you change the way, you look at things, and look at them from God's perspective with thankfulness and hope, the things you look at will change.

PRAYER

God, You are good so there is good everywhere You are. Help me see the good, the benefit and the blessing in every breath.

I want to remember and work on ......

I heard God say ......

CRY IF YOU WANT TO

Those who sow in tears shall reap with shouts of joy.
Psalm 126:5 ESV

Trials are coming, and nobody said you can't feel some kind of way about them. You do know you are allowed to cry, right? The Bible says weeping may endure for a night, but joy comes in the morning. It also says there is a time and a season for everything, and that includes time for crying. Crying is most definitely okay and many times necessary.

Even though God works everything out for your good, that certainly does not mean you will always feel good about everything that is going on while He is working it out. Be real; sometimes you feel sad, angry, frustrated, misunderstood, tired, depressed, hurt, lonely, unappreciated, used, or just plain ole worn out. I normally feel better after a good cry, so I did some research to let you know the benefits of crying. Men, you can cry, too; it's okay.

Crying is a healthy way to let out pent-up emotions, relieve stress, detoxify the body, lessen the pain, cope with loss, and sometimes crying is a way to demonstrate unspeakable joy. When you need a good cry, give yourself a full day to let it out; your body, mind and spirit will thank you. Be good to yourself, you deserve it.

PRAYER

God, thank You for allowing me to release my emotions and know that everything You make is good. Thank You for Your comfort as I cry. Thank You for helping me realize crying is a great way for me to lighten my load and rest because I am not on anyone's schedule. Thank You for making me beautiful in my own time.

I want to remember and work on ......

I heard God say ......

DON'T GET DISTRACTED

Watch out for people that try to dazzle you with big words and influential
double talk. They want to drag you off into
endless arguments that never amount to nothing.
Colossians 2:8 MSG

As we live out our God given calling, we will have detours, roadblocks, and pit stops, but keep moving forward anyway. Sometimes, you will have to talk to yourself and say, "Stay focused, you got this," or if God brought you to it, he'll get you through it." I like to put pictures of my goals on the wall to remind me of what I want to accomplish.

Make sure you protect your purpose, and don't let people talk to you about stuff that's not productive because what you focus on can affect your forward progress. Staying focused could involve taking a break from other people's issues, opinions, and ideas or taking a sabbatical to be silent and hear from God. It could also mean limiting time with people, places, and things that take you off the path God has for you. Do not wait until the fear is gone, or else you will not go through the doors God opens. Let nothing and no one stop or deter you from your divine assignment.

PRAYER

Lord, please give me the wisdom, discernment, and strength to block out the noise as I continuously follow Your lead.

I want to remember and work on ......

I heard God say ......

DREAM BIGGER

Therefore, I tell you, whatever you ask for in prayer, believe that you have received it, and it will be yours.
Mark 11:24 NLT

Are you living the life you've always imagined? If not, what's stopping you? Before moving to Florida, I would feel sad during the winter months because I was often in the house more due to the cold, rainy, and icy weather. I heard most of my life that Washington, DC, was the place to be for the young, gifted, and Black, but my life vision was always living in a warm place with sun and palm trees while wearing shorts and sandals. So, with God's help, my husband and I packed our bags and moved to Florida.

I am sure you have a dream too. Get out of your comfort zone and dream as big as you want. Do not worry about how big the task. You do not need permission from anyone. God has the power to give you the desires of your heart. Someone once said if your dream is something you can do without God, then your dream is not big enough.

PRAYER

God, I believe nothing is too hard for you, so I fully surrender my wants, needs, desires, and dreams to you.

ENCOURAGEMENT

I want to remember and work on ......

I heard God say ......

FORGIVE AND LET IT GO

Be tolerant with each other and, if someone has a complaint against anyone,
forgive each other. As the Lord forgave you, so also forgive each other.
Colossians 3:13 CEB

Make sure that nobody pays back wrong for wrong but always strives to do
what is good for each other and everyone else.
1 Thessalonians 5:15 NIV

When you hold on to all the times you've been hurt and all the people who have hurt you or all the stuff you regret, it's hard to move forward. Holding on to the bad stuff can be stressful and painful, keep you stuck, and make you sick. Pack light and do just as it says in Psalm 24:19, *"Don't be mad when the evil are blessed."*

I always thought forgiveness was like saying I am ok with people's mistreatment of me or not forgiving me was my punishment for not giving God my best. With much growth and prayer, I realized you forgive because God tells you to forgive, you forgive because you want to be forgiven, you forgive because nobody is perfect, you forgive because not forgiving is like a cancer that destroys your body, mind, peace, and joy and lastly, you forgive because God forgave you. God's grace and mercy are brand new every day, so stop beating yourself up about the past and let others off the hook too. Today is a new day to enjoy.

PRAYER

God, thank You for always forgiving me. Please help me give the same grace and forgiveness to others.

I want to remember and work on ......

I heard God say ......

GET REALLY EXCITED
ABOUT TODAY

This is the day that the Lord has made, let us rejoice and be glad in it.
Psalm 118:24 ESV

Y ou are a good and perfect gift from God, created with God given gifts and talents that never expire! So, if you have a slow start or get turned around, remember it is not about how you start but how you finish.

Khadeja Williams had been homeless since age 6, but even though she lived on the street and in shelters, she had faith, kept studying and stayed on top of her school requirements. She was determined not to let her current circumstances stop her from achieving her goals. She got up at 4 am to catch several buses to get to school. Her high grades helped her get accepted to over 20 colleges and universities. She accepted a scholarship, attended, and graduated from Harvard University. Now, she inspires and helps kids in tough situations dream big and achieve their dreams.

Good things are always happening because nothing is impossible with God. But if you get a little scared, Matthew 18:19 (NIV) says, *"Get a friend, and if you agree on anything you ask for, it will be done."*

PRAYER

Lord, thank You for today, for making it great, and for giving me everything I need.

I want to remember and work on ......

I heard God say ......

GET SOME GOOD FRIENDS

A friend loves you all the time, and a brother helps in times of trouble.

Proverbs 17:17 NCV

When I was having some health challenges and had gone to many doctors, but still suffering, my friend asked if we could fast and pray. I cried because she was willing to turn down her plate and not eat to seek God for an answer to my problem. Now that's a friend! We fasted and prayed for a month, and God gave us the answer.

Here's another example: When my family moved to Florida from Washington, DC, we left everyone behind. We had no friends or family in Miami. I craved sisterhood and friendship. Video calls were no longer cutting it. I prayed and asked God to send me some friends. Now, I did not want just any ole friends. My prayer was specific. I asked for friends I could trust with my heart: my husband, my son, and my God.

I asked for friends I could pray with and grow with, who loved me, respected me, supported me, and let me be myself. I would do the same for them. Oprah said, "Lots of people want to ride with you in the limo, but what you want is someone that will take the bus with you when the limo breaks down." God is your source for everything so ask him for what you want and need, including new friends.

111

PRAYER

God, surround me with the people You send, friends I can enjoy life with, people I can love and that will love me even when I'm not at my best.

I want to remember and work on ......

I heard God say ......

GET SOME HELP

Your word is a lamp for my feet, a light on my path.
Psalm 119:105

Those who love me, I will deliver; I will protect those who know my name.
When they call me, I will answer them; I will be with them in trouble, I will
rescue them and honor them.
Psalm 91:14-15 NRSV

I have often heard people say the Bible stands for Basic Instructions for Before Leaving Earth although God never gave the Bible this tittle, the Bible is an important resource for knowing God, loving God, and loving you. The bible has something in it that can help you no matter what is happening. Although it was written over 2,000 years ago the insight contained in it is still valuable and relatable for everyday living.

The bible gives insight on God's character and His purpose which can help you trust God and discover not only His love, but the power He has given you to live a live that He purposed. If your body was sick you would go to the doctor to try to get medicine that will help you feel better well God's word, the Bible is the ultimate assistance, benefit, and support for whatever you need.

Here are a few scriptures to get you going in the right direction:
1. Need encouragement. John 3:16

2. Dealing with Fear. Psalm 347
3. Feeling discouraged. Romans 8:31
4. Want happiness. Colossians 3:12-17
5. Looking for peace. Matthew 11:28-30
6. Worried. Matthew 6:19-34
7. In need of healing. Jeremiah 17:14

PRAYER

Lord I cannot live my life without You. Help me understand Your word and use it as the source of all the answers I need.

I want to remember and work on ......

I heard God say ......

LEAD WITH LOVE

My dear, dear friends, if God loved us like this,
we certainly ought to love each other.
1 John 4:11-12 MSG

God tells us to do 2 things - Love God and Love others as we love Ourselves. Paul says these requirements cover all ten of the commandments, so love God, love you, and love people.

Sometimes, we are not so nice in how we speak to us about us or what we say to others. Sometimes, I must catch myself saying negative stuff to me about me. When I look in the mirror, I'm often critical of me. This is too big, this is too small, this should be flatter, my hair is a mess, why did I do that again? We are to be patient, gentle and loving not only to others but also to ourselves.

To be honest, this scripture covers everything: your thoughts, your words, and your actions. So, before you think, say, or do anything, start it with love. It might feel weird at first, and I would be lying if I said it's always easy to do, but God isn't asking you to do this from your own power; He will help you every step of the way.

PRAYER

God, You know I'm a work in progress, so before I open my mouth or take one step, help me, lead me, and give me the strength to do everything with love.

ENCOURAGEMENT

I want to remember and work on ......

I heard God say ......

LET THEM TALK

To you who are ready for the truth, I say this: Love your enemies. Let them bring out the best in you, not the worst. When someone gives you a hard time, respond with the supple moves of prayer for that person.
Luke 6:27-28 MSG

Not everyone will agree with your assignment, your dreams, your goals, or how you show up in the world. People might say you will never amount to anything, you should give up, it will never work, or you don't deserve it. When God gives you an assignment, you do not need permission or approval from anyone to move in the direction of it.

Haters are gonna hate; that's what they do, and yes it can and will sometimes hurt. You might not always feel like going high when they go low, like Michelle Obama said, but you should do what God says and not mistreat anyone, even those who hurt you. Yes, even those that lie on you, lie to you, or mistreat you.

However, even though you don't retaliate or clap back when people do mean things to you or talk negatively about you it does not mean they get a front row seat in your life. You are well within your rights to minimize your time or disconnect from them. I like what Mandy Hale said, "Don't waste words on people who deserve your silence. Sometimes, the most powerful thing you can say is nothing at all."

PRAYER

God, sometimes I need a little extra help to let my thoughts and actions represent you. Block out the noise of anything that is not from you. As You block it out, I will walk it out.

I want to remember and work on ......

I heard God say ......

MAKE EVERY DAY AN ADVENTURE

Always be joyful because you belong to the Lord. I will say it again, be joyful!
Philippians 4:4 NIRV

Jesus said, "*I came that they may have and enjoy life, and have it in abundance (to the full, till it overflows)*" John 10:10 (AMPC). That means enjoy life now; don't wait for a specific day or time. I have entered some churches, and I say to myself, if these people have Jesus, each breath is a blessing, and the joy of the Lord is our strength, then why do so many people look like they just sucked a bag of lemons? People, it's okay to smile, be happy, and enjoy your life.

Each day is an opportunity to talk to God, walk with God, hear from God, enjoy God, be close with God, experience His love, His peace, His comfort, as well as get His direction and protection as you learn from His wisdom. God has already given you everything you need to live an amazing life. Don't force anything or try to make things happen on your own. Ask for what you want and need, throw away your due dates, and trust God's guidance and His timing as you happily and fully enjoy your journey.

PRAYER

God no matter what is happening, help me to enjoy every breath you give.

ENCOURAGEMENT

I want to remember and work on ......

I heard God say ......

MIND YOUR BUSINESS

I know that there is nothing better for people than to be happy and to do good while they live. That each of them may eat and drink and find satisfaction in all their toil—this is the gift of God.
Ecclesiastes 3:12-13 NIV

God made you for a reason with something special and specific to do that will benefit the world. Whatever God wants you to do is just the right fit for your personality, your gifts and talents, and your experiences. You don't have to feel unworthy of the assignment, worry about forcing yourself to fit into the current culture or doing what's already been done. God is doing a new thing.

I heard Steven Furtick preach about being a bird in a fishbowl by trying to be someone or something you are not. He said, "he was always in trouble at school for talking, and his teacher told him, no one is going to pay money to listen to you talk all day." But God! Now he uses his voice to preach, teach, inspire and encourage millions of people around the world. Your soul knows you're a teacher, builder, warrior, author, preacher, leader, encourager, designer, dancer, artist, or _____. You fill in the blank. Tomorrow is not promised, so be unapologetically you, every day, all day.

PRAYER

God, give me the wisdom, confidence, and strength to live happily and boldly the life you designed for me. You anointed, appointed, and approved me for my assignment so help me to not seek approval from others but consciously commit to following your lead.

I want to remember and work on ......

I heard God say ......

PRAISE GOD NO MATTER WHAT

Rejoice always, pray constantly, give thanks in all circumstances;
for this is the will of God in Christ Jesus.
1 Thessalonians 5:14-18 NIV

In life, you will face trials, not that you might but you will at some point be in some not so great situations and circumstances. The book, "The Hiding Place" tells the story of 2 Dutch Christian sisters who helped harbor Jews from the Nazis in Holland during World War 2. The sisters were arrested and imprisoned in a German concentration camp.

They and hundreds of women were prisoners, sick, hungry, and given dirty straw platforms infested with fleas to sleep on. They found a way to sneak in a bible and came upon this passage. Even though imprisoned, they included their captors in their prayer of thanks. They even thanked God for the fleas. Although inspections occurred daily in the camp, the guards never inspected their prison.

The women eventually found out the guards never inspected their area because they didn't want to be bitten by the diseased fleas, get sick, or die. Remember praise is your prayer, praise is your peace, praise is your weapon, praise is your power, praise is your thank you, and praise is your amen.

PRAYER

God, I thank You for protecting and keeping me, even from the dangers I am unwilling or cannot see.

I want to remember and work on ......

I heard God say ......

PRAY ABOUT EVERYTHING!!

Don't worry about anything; instead, pray about everything.
Tell God what you need and thank him for all he has done.
Philippians 4:6-7 NLT

Prayer is our communion, our communication, and our connection with God. It's not one-way communication where we do all the talking and God does all the listening, but it's two-way, where we talk then listen for God's dialog to us. The Bible says we should pray about everything. Nothing is too big or too small, and we should pray all the time and never stop praying.

So, pray when you're happy, pray when you're happy, pray when you're sad, pray when you're sick, pray when you're hurting, pray when you're confused, pray when you're in trouble, pray when you need answers, pray for strength, pray for those that hurt you, pray for direction, pray for protection, pray for abundance, pray for peace and pray a prayer of thanks for all God is, all He has done and all He will do. Pray about everything! Did you know God does not grade or critique our prayers? So, your prayers do not have to be twenty minutes or as long as a book. Prayer can be short, quick, and simple like God help me or God thank you. Whatever the prayer, God hears you.

PRAYER

God, I know You can handle whatever I have going on because nothing is impossible with You by my side. Let me not be afraid or embarrassed about anything. Help me trust You with my heart so I talk to You about everything with nothing being off limits. I'm putting my trust in You. Thank You for never turning Your back on me and for always being such an amazing listener.

I want to remember and work on ......

I heard God say ......

PROTECT YOUR PEACE

May the Lord of peace himself give you peace always in every way.
The Lord be with you all.
2 Thessalonians 3:16 CEB

Being at peace reminds me of the story of Joseph in Genesis 37 in the Bible. His siblings were jealous and did not like him much. Their dislike was so extreme that they threw him into a pit, and eventually sold him into slavery. The Bible doesn't say Joseph wasted a lot of time and energy being angry about how badly his family mistreated him or any brain cells on seeking revenge.

What it does say is when he eventually saw his brothers many years later, he did not curse them or hurt them but showed them love, kindness, and favor. He gave them land and food, but he sure didn't invite them to live with him in the palace. He gave them their own space, their own place, and loved them from a distance.

God calls us to live in peace with everyone, and sometimes, that means decreasing the amount of time spent with them. You are under no obligation to live with, take phone calls, go out to lunch, answer texts, or like posts of people who don't love and honor you. Your life, your sanity, and your peace are precious and worth protecting.

PRAYER

Lord, help me appreciate the peace You give and help me not allow anyone to diminish, dismantle, or destroy it.

I want to remember and work on ......

I heard God say ......

REMEMBER THE VISION

And the LORD answered me: "Write the vision; make it plain on tablets,
so he may run who reads it.
Habakkuk 2:2 ESV

D o you have goals you want to accomplish? Goals like buying a house, finishing school, getting married, starting a family, starting a new job, writing a book, or opening a business? Then it is more than likely you have a vision for where you want to be and what you want to achieve. The vision helps you see, plan, and carry out the steps needed to accomplish your goals. Just like you have things you want to do in life, God has things He created you to accomplish too. If you did not know, you are here to do great things for which God has purposed you to do before you were born. You're not on this earth just to suck up air.

God has something important for you to do and the vision God has for your life and the assignments you complete will glorify Him. The good news is you won't have to do it all by yourself, God will surely help. God gives you the desires of you heart and prayerfully as you spend more time with Him, your desires align with His. As it says in Proverbs 19:9 NLT, *"we can make our plans, but the LORD determines our steps."*

Trust your plan to God, write it down, make it plain then keep moving in the direction of it. Each day do one thing to move you forward. Do not compare your progress to anyone else. Your one thing can be to pray, make a call, send a text, do some research, read a book, take a class, visualize, meditate, or talk positively to you about it. Trust God to direct your steps, open the right doors and send His divine resources.

PRAYER

Lord steady my mind, my body, my talk, my actions and my attitude on the vision You designed and course you set.

I want to remember and work on ......

I heard God say ......

SAY THANK YOU

Rejoice always, pray continually, give thanks in all circumstances; for this is God's will for you in Christ Jesus.
1 Thessalonians 5:16-18 NIV

Saying thank you is your demonstration of gratitude to God. Thank you, helps you realize who God is and shows your appreciation of His blessings. Gratitude helps you reduce stress, worry, and anxiety because you are focused on the good things. Saying thanks is a way to let God know you trust Him and believe He is working everything out for your good, which results in peace. Research shows people who are grateful and express appreciation are more joyful, have fewer sick days and have greater satisfaction in life

There are so many things to thank God for, like life, strength, and hope, as well as his love, kindness, grace, mercy, power, wisdom, help, and comfort. I could fill up an entire page with things to thank God for. So, thank God by showing gratitude for who He is, what He's done, what He's going to do, for all that you are, all that you have, and for His best, that's on the way.

PRAYER

God, thank you for your everything even the stuff the negative stuff because I know You will use it all for my good.

ENCOURAGEMENT

I want to remember and work on ......

I heard God say ......

SAY YES

*And I heard the voice of the Lord saying, "Whom shall I send, and who will
go for us?" Then I said, "Here I am! Send me."*
Isaiah 6:8 NIV

God has a plan and a purpose for you that only you can complete. Your God assignment never expires. If you have breath in your body, it's yours. However, God will never force you to take the assignment. It reminds me of the James Bond 007 movies. James gets an assignment, but it does not begin until he chooses to accept it. The good thing about God's assignment is that it's not to harm you but to prosper you, to give you hope and a future. Nobody can give you a promise like that other than God.

Whatever the assignment God gives, do it just like it says in Colossians 3:23 (NLT), "*Work willingly at whatever you do, as though you were doing it for the Lord, rather than people.*" Do everything with excellence as if God's name is on it.

Live with excellence and integrity, operate with excellence and integrity, move with excellence and integrity, think with excellence and integrity, communicate with excellence and integrity, work with excellence and integrity, and treat people with excellence and integrity. Be excellent in everything!

133

PRAYER

God, I am here to be the light in this world and represent you with all my being. Please help me to do my best and represent you with 100% excellence in everything.

I want to remember and work on ......

I heard God say ......

SEEK GOD FIRST

*Seek the Kingdom of God above all else, and live righteously,
and he will give you everything you need.*
Matthew 6:33 NLT

The Bible says to seek God first; then the rest will come. Most often when you want to have a great relationship with someone, you talk to them, you look at their social media, you think about them, you want to see them, you keep pictures of them where you can see them, and you make plans with them in mind. We put time, energy, effort, and thought into making the relationship and our interactions enjoyable. You're happy with anticipation for the next meeting, the next text, or the next call because you value who they are, what they have to say, and what they mean in your life.

If you take that much care to develop relationships with people, be willing to go the extra mile and make the effort to have an amazing relationship with God, your creator and source of everything good.

I enjoy morning walks in my neighborhood on weekends because most people are asleep, there is little to no traffic so the walk is quiet, and I can hear God better. One day, as I was walking and talking to God, I asked him to let me know He was still there. As I was looking down at my feet just as I had finished the question, a leaf fell from the tree right in front of my face. It reminded me that God always knows where I am. He cares about me and my life, and He's available if I just take the time to pay attention and look for Him.

PRAYER

God, You have the answer for any and all of my questions. God help me seek you first not just once in the morning but throughout the day. Unclutter my mind, my thoughts and my schedule so I can live, truly live my life with You at the center, my first priority before anything or anyone else.

I want to remember and work on ......

I heard God say ......

SHARE GOD WITH OTHERS

Oh give thanks to the LORD; call upon his name; make known his deeds among the peoples!
1 Chronicles 16:8 ESV

Have you ever heard someone share your testimony? That word testimony might be a little too churchy or make you feel obligated to share God in ways that feel forced, or it might scare you, but don't be scared, it just means share your story. Tell someone, anyone about the goodness of God. Just do it naturally and if you need help to share how good God has been to you, just ask Him to give you courage.

Communicate what you love about God or call a friend and give an update on what's good. We share so much of ourselves online and in our personal conversations, why not talk about how God woke you up, healed your body or even kept you from going off on the person that cut you off in traffic.

Sharing helps you remember the good stuff, sharing helps others see the realness and relevance of God as a loving father and friend who never leaves, always protects and is the source for everything they need. There is a lady at our neighborhood pool who always shares her story with anyone that listens that she was not supposed to be there. How her life and her ability to walk and talk are just a few of God's miracles in her life. You see, she had many strokes, one after the other and was on life support but God healed her body, and the only evidence of the strokes is a limp on her right side. She can lower herself into the pool unassisted and is even taking swimming lessons.

So, the next time you feel the need to give someone hope or brighten their day, tell them in your own words how good God has been to you and watch it not only give them hope but help you remember how great God has been and still is.

PRAYER

God thank You for always being with me, for helping me, guiding me and loving me. Help me to not be afraid to happily share you with others.

I want to remember and work on ......

I heard God say ......

SIT YOUR BUTT DOWN AND LISTEN

Come to me, all you who are weary and burdened, and I will give you rest.
Matthew 11:28 NIV

We can be extremely busy. It's like we wear busyness as a badge of honor. We are so focused on doing the next big thing: completing a project, helping a friend, serving at church, taking care of the kids, going to school, cleaning the house, looking for a mate, or getting our lives in order that we miss what God is saying. There is always something we must do, which can be overwhelming. It's like time is your enemy, always pushing you to do more, to be more, or to add something else to your plate.

Even as God was creating the world, He rested on the 7th day, and you need rest too. Rest and silence give you time to hear from God, as well as replenish and rejuvenate for your journey ahead. Do not be fooled, rest is required for a healthy, happy life, Sadly, you might feel guilty or be called lazy when you take time to stop and do nothing but do not give in to guilt. Your life and wellbeing matter to God. Lao Tzo said, "To the mind that is still, the whole universe surrenders."

PRAYER

God, let me hear You as I surrender my schedule. I am Yours. Have Your way and let me hear Your still small voice as I unplug from the noise of life.

Be front and center as I take time to rest, relax, refill, restore, and refocus so I do what matters most.

I want to remember and work on ......

I heard God say ......

TAKE TIME TO CARE FOR YOU

Casting all your anxieties on him, because he cares for you.
1 Peter 5:7 ESV

Jesus is the savior of the world, not you so it's ok to stop being the go-to person who solves everyone's problems. When you are on a plane, and there is a problem, if oxygen is needed, you are told to put your oxygen mask on before trying to help anyone. God never asked you to save anyone or fix yours or other people's problems. I used to take pride in being called the fixer, but as I was fixing everyone's mess, I was sick, tired, stressed, and overwhelmed as a result. Can someone please get Jesus on the mainline because He is the only fixer we need! Not only is He everywhere, He knows everything and has all the power with unlimited resources and solutions to handle the situation.

Take time for self-care or get in some me time so you can rest and be healthy spiritually, physically, emotionally, and mentally. Give yourself time and space to breathe. Research shows just 5 minutes of quiet per day can help you sleep better, reduce stress, increase clarity, grow in compassion, and be in a space to hear what God has to say.

Caring for you should include taking time to eat food that fuels your body, exercising, and getting adequate amounts of rest. Self-care is not a luxury, but it is a well deserved necessity.

PRAYER

Lord, let me remember I matter to You too. I am not a second-class citizen and it's not only okay but essential that I take time to care for the mind, body, and soul that You so generously gave me. Give me peace and joy as I find rest, renewal, and strength in You.

I want to remember and work on ......

I heard God say ......

TELL THE TRUTH

Better is the poor who walks in his integrity, than one who is
perverse in his lips, and is a fool.
Proverbs 19:1 NKJV

Have you ever been in a situation where you thought a lie would be the best solution? Don't judge me, but when I was younger, I purchased a jumpsuit from the department store. It was sooooooo cute in the store, but when I got home to try it on, I realized it was too small and tried to squeeze myself into it, and the zipper broke.

Immediately, I am almost ashamed to admit it, but my first thought was to take it back to the store and pretend it was broken when I bought it. But I know telling a lie, even a lie of omission, would not be God-like behavior, so I didn't take it back and learned a $40 lesson. If I want to be God's example, then I must do things God's way. Although I did the right thing that time, my Godly walk has been and is still a work in progress.

Do your best to act, speak, and live in ways that positively reflect God. Let the Holy Spirit help you by showing you the way. If you don't get it right the first time, don't beat yourself up; ask for God's wisdom and guidance and do better the next time.

PRAYER

God, teach me Your ways and give me the strength and courage to do what's right even when it's not comfortable or popular.

I want to remember and work on ......

I heard God say ......

THINK ABOUT THE GOOD STUFF

In conclusion, my friends fill your minds with those things that are good
and that deserve praise; things that are true, noble, right,
pure, lovely, and honorable.
Phil 4:8 GNT

I often hear people say you get what you expect or what you focus on gows. All your thoughts, actions, reactions, fears, negative emotions, compromises, and disappointments can become your daily reality if that's all you think about. You can focus on all the bad stuff, all the things not working, with all the stuff that needs to be done and become obsessed, stressed, and depressed, or you can do as God says and focus on what's good.

God has given you good things to occupy your thoughts like you are more than a conqueror, you are God's masterpiece, God is always with you, God never gives up on you, nothing is impossible with God, God is your safe place in times of trouble, and God will work everything out for your good no matter the situation. How about focusing on how powerful you are because you have the same power that raised Jesus from the dead, inside of you.

Why not focus on how God allows you to ask, and it will be given to you. If you seek you will find or if you keep on knocking the door will be opened to you? You are tremendously loved and blessed. Dron't waste another second

145

on a thought that does not serve you or is not in your best interest.

PRAYER

God help me to forget what is behind me, let go of the negative and spend my time and energy pressing forward to achieve the plans and goals You have for me as I keep my attention on what's good.

I want to remember and work on ......

I heard God say ......

WAIT ON GOD

Trust in the LORD with all your heart; do not depend on your own understanding. Seek his will in all you do, and he will show you which path to take.
Proverbs 3:5-6 NLT

Before I was married, in my heart, I knew I was tired of dating. I was ready to share my life with the man God had for me. A husband I could share my life with so I went to work and Got busy talking to God and doing what He said. I prayed, meditated, journaled, sat quietly, read the Bible, read spiritual books, turned off the television, went to women's conferences and retreats, as well as rested as I made myself available to hear from God. I looked for Him every day, several times a day. I wanted to hear His still, small voice, so I slowed down, made room, and took time to hear Him so I could do what He said.

Look at your daily schedule; do you prioritize spending time with God or is every moment filled and cluttered with stuff that could be given a lower importance, priority, or significance? Do you spend more than one or two minutes in the morning or before bed talking to God? Are you even listening or are you just talking? Where do you spend most of your time? Is it with family, working, having fun, or serving in too many ministries at church? Even too much of a good thing can keep you from hearing God and going where and when He leads.

PRAYER

Honestly, God I have not made the best choices with the time You have given me. Help me not miss the road signs You've posted by putting You first before anyone and anything.

I want to remember and work on ......

I heard God say ......

WALK EVEN WHEN YOU CAN'T SEE

For no word from God will ever fail.
Luke 1:37 NIV

I love reading and listening to the daily motivational words of some of my favorite scriptures. One I have on my office wall is "Faith does not make things easy; it makes them possible," which is based on this scripture.

The Bible says faith without works is dead, so faith is the evidence, the belief, the action you take to move forward, to stay focused, and to stay on purpose even when or if you can't see God working it out. Faith demonstrates the trust you have in your Heavenly Father to hear your prayers and do what's best. Sometimes walking by faith can seem like it happens at the worst time when you are calling God because you are in distress and in desperate need of help or solutions.

Do you have the faith and patience to wait when you have no answers and no one else to go to for help, you have prayed and prayed, and God has yet to answer? Some call this a desert experience. It's called a desert experience because during these times it can appear and feel like you are in a dry and desolate place devoid of help now and no help coming soon. When you are in a desert experience, you will have no other options but to totally rely on God.

Demonstrating your faith can be done in a variety of ways like praying, meditating, reading scripture, researching

149

God's word, making a call, sending a text, or totally taking your hands off the situation, trusting God and listening for God's guidance and direction. If you know no word from God will ever fail, what's stopping you from taking a step forward each day to go where God is leading?

PRAYER

Faithful God, please lay an extra hand of wisdom and guidance on me so every step I take aligns with the plans You have for me.

I want to remember and work on ......

I heard God say ......

CONCLUSION

Before you go, please read Proverbs 3:5-12 the Message version. It sums up how to live a life that honors God and all He created you to be.

"Trust God from the bottom of your heart; don't try to figure out everything on your own. Listen for God's voice in everything you do, everywhere you go; he's the one who will keep you on track.

Don't assume you know it all. Run to God! Run from evil! Your body will glow with health, your very bones will vibrate with life! Honor God with everything you own; give him the first and the best. Your barns will burst, your wine vats will brim over.

But don't dear friend, resent God's discipline; don't sulk under his loving correction. It's the child he loves that God corrects; a father's delight is behind all this. The Very Tree of Life."

I pray you spend time with God, seek His face continually, trust Him at his word and enjoy every moment of every day because Sunday Ain't Enough to build a loving relationship with the one who loves you most.

XOXO,

Dr. Carolyn

LET'S PRAY

God, wherever we go, let there be a shift, a change in the atmosphere. You called us with a specific purpose to accomplish. As we grow, evolve, and mature, let us know you, trust you, and love you. Let us believe everything you say about us, everything you say we can have, everything you say we can do, and everything you say we can be. Thank you in advance for all you do to and through us.

In Jesus' mighty and marvelous name, Amen.

I WOULD LOVE TO
CONNECT WITH YOU!

@drcarolynedwards

www.drcarolynedwards.com
www.sundayaintenough.com

Help other readers find this book:
- Post a review online or on social media.
- Post a picture and share why you enjoy it.
- Send a note to a friend who would also love it or send them a copy.
- Request a copy be included in your local library.

ALSO AVAILABLE FROM

DR. CAROLYN EDWARDS

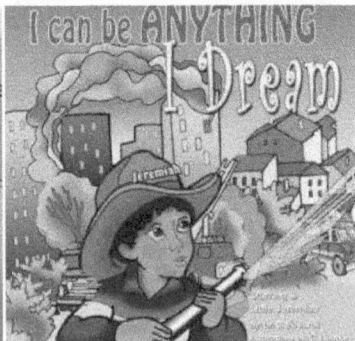

I LOOK GOOD
I FEEL GOOD
I AM GOOD

THE WOMAN'S GUIDE TO
LOVE, PEACE AND HAPPINESS

DR. CAROLYN EDWARDS

Teach ONLINE
10 Simple Steps to Get Your Résumé Noticed
and Land the Job

DR. CAROLYN EDWARDS

FUN with MONEY

I can be ANYTHING I Dream

www.ingramcontent.com/pod-product-compliance
Lightning Source LLC
Chambersburg PA
CBHW021953090426
42811CB00001B/5